Why Dogs Are Better Than Men

JENNIFER BERMAN

POCKET BOOKS

New York   London   Toronto   Sydney   Tokyo   Singapore

For orders other than by individual consumers, Pocket Books grants a discount on the purchase of **10 or more** copies of single titles for special markets or premium use. For further details, please write to the Vice-President of Special Markets, Pocket Books, 1633 Broadway, New York, NY 10019-6785, 8th Floor.

For information on how individual consumers can place orders, please write to Mail Order Department, Simon & Schuster Inc., 200 Old Tappan Road, Old Tappan, NJ 07675.

A few of the cartoons in this book have appeared as postcards. Jennifer Berman's postcards are available from Humerus Cartoons, P.O. Box 6614, Evanston, IL 60204-6614.

An *Original* Publication of POCKET BOOKS

POCKET BOOKS, a division of Simon & Schuster Inc.
1230 Avenue of the Americas, New York, NY 10020

Copyright © 1993 by Jennifer Berman
Front cover illustration by Jennifer Berman

ISBN: 0-671-86488-2

First Pocket Books trade paperback printing November 1993

10 9 8 7 6 5 4

Pocket and colophon are registered trademarks of Simon & Schuster Inc.

Printed in the U.S.A.

This book is for any woman who has steadfastly resisted the frequent urge to feloniously resolve her relationship with our hormonally challenged counterparts. In his excellent book *Punchlines,* William Keough has a flow chart that illustrates the critical role of humor in our society:

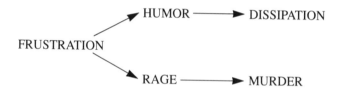

So it is in the interests of lightening the load on our already overburdened court system that I offer this book. Because without humor, nothing would be funny.

Acknowledgments

Thanks to the following humans:

Eric Bates, a giant among friends; Benjamin Horowitz, for all those shreds of paper you sent me when you should have been thinking about personal autonomy; Emily Budziak Williams, my spiritual twin; Amy Gelband MacDonald, for the unconditional laughter; Bucky Halker, for all the inspirational cups of coffee and merciless ribbing; Eric Tobias, mensch and editor par excellence; Jeremy Solomon, crack agent; Debra McQueen, Nicole Hollander, Nicole Ferentz, and Tom Greensfelder, for being so generous with space and friendship and not saying anything about all the dog hair; and my family, for either believing in me or being polite enough not to say anything too discouraging at critical moments.

Thanks to the following nonhumans:

Lyka and Isaac, whose magnificent, unself-conscious capacity for love, zeal for squirrel-chasing, and ardor for fun keep things in proper perspective for me. Good dogs.

And thanks to Maggie, who, already horrified by having to share her home with one slobbering furball, graciously embraced the arrival of Dog Number Two, without extricating any eyeballs from their original sockets. Nice kitty.

Chapter One

WHY DOGS ARE BETTER THAN MEN

DOGS DO NOT HAVE PROBLEMS EXPRESSING AFFECTION IN PUBLIC

DOGS MISS YOU WHEN YOU'RE GONE

YOU NEVER WONDER WHETHER YOUR DOG IS GOOD ENOUGH FOR YOU

DOGS FEEL GUILT WHEN THEY'VE DONE SOMETHING WRONG

DOGS DON'T BRAG ABOUT WHOM THEY HAVE SLEPT WITH

DOGS DON'T CRITICIZE YOUR FRIENDS

WHAT HE THINKS OF YOUR FRIENDS:
- A TERRIBLY INSECURE
- B INCOMPREHENSIBLE
- C TOO PERFECT
- D TOO CRITICAL
- E TOO AFFECTED
- F SHALLOW

WHAT YOUR DOG THINKS:
- A NICE!
- B GREAT TASTE IN CLOTHES!
- C NICE!
- D NICE!
- E NICE!
- F NICE!

DOGS ADMIT WHEN THEY'RE JEALOUS

DOGS ARE VERY DIRECT ABOUT WANTING TO GO OUT

DOGS DO NOT PLAY GAMES WITH YOU—EXCEPT FETCH
(AND THEY NEVER LAUGH AT HOW YOU THROW)

DOGS ARE HAPPY WITH ANY VIDEO YOU CHOOSE TO RENT, because they know the most important thing is that you're together

DOGS DON'T FEEL THREATENED BY YOUR INTELLIGENCE

NO DOG EVER VOTED TO CONFIRM CLARENCE THOMAS

YOU CAN TRAIN A DOG

DOGS ARE EASY TO BUY FOR

DOGS ARE GOOD WITH KIDS

DOGS ARE ALREADY IN TOUCH WITH THEIR INNER PUPPIES

YOU ARE NEVER SUSPICIOUS OF YOUR DOG'S DREAMS

GORGEOUS DOGS DON'T KNOW THEY'RE GORGEOUS

THE WORST SOCIAL DISEASE YOU CAN GET FROM DOGS IS FLEAS*

* OK. THE <u>REALLY</u> WORST DISEASE YOU CAN GET FROM THEM IS RABIES, BUT THERE'S A VACCINE FOR IT, AND YOU GET TO KILL THE ONE WHO GIVES IT TO YOU.

DOGS UNDERSTAND WHAT <u>NO</u> MEANS....

DOGS DON'T NEED THERAPY TO UNDO THEIR BAD SOCIALIZATION

NO DOG EVER WORKED ON THE MANHATTAN PROJECT

DOGS DON'T MAKE A PRACTICE OF KILLING THEIR OWN SPECIES

DALMATIAN   RUSSIAN WOLFHOUND   GERMAN SHEPHERD   PEKINGESE

DOGS UNDERSTAND IF SOME OF THEIR FRIENDS CANNOT COME INSIDE

DOGS DO NOT READ AT THE TABLE

YOU CAN HOUSE-TRAIN A DOG

YOU CAN FORCE A DOG TO TAKE A BATH

DOGS KNOW YOU HAVE BRILLIANT TASTE IN MUSIC (and a voice to match!)

MIDDLE-AGED DOGS DON'T FEEL THE NEED TO ABANDON YOU FOR A YOUNGER OWNER

DOGS AREN'T THREATENED BY A WOMAN WITH SHORT HAIR

DOGS AREN'T THREATENED BY TWO WOMEN WITH SHORT HAIR

DOGS DON'T MIND IF YOU DO ALL THE DRIVING

DOGS DON'T STEP ON THE IMAGINARY BRAKE

DOGS ADMIT IT WHEN THEY'RE LOST

DOGS DON'T WEIGH DOWN YOUR PURSE WITH THEIR STUFF

DOGS LOOK AT YOUR EYES

DOGS LIKE YOUR SIZE

DOGS DO NOT CARE WHETHER YOU SHAVE YOUR LEGS

DOGS TAKE CARE OF THEIR OWN NEEDS

DOGS ARE COLOR-BLIND

NO DOG IS A MEMBER OF THE N.R.A.

DOGS AREN'T THREATENED IF YOU EARN MORE THAN THEY DO

DOGS <u>MEAN</u> IT WHEN THEY KISS YOU

DOGS ARE NICE TO YOUR RELATIVES

DOGS OBSESS ABOUT YOU AS MUCH AS YOU OBSESS ABOUT THEM

Chapter Two

HOW DOGS AND MEN ARE THE SAME

BOTH TAKE UP TOO MUCH SPACE ON THE BED

BOTH ARE THREATENED BY THEIR OWN KIND

BOTH LIKE TO CHEW WOOD

IT DOESN'T TAKE A DOG THREE HOURS TO TAKE A DUMP....

BUT AT LEAST MEN DON'T DO IT RIGHT IN FRONT OF THE NEIGHBORS

BOTH MARK THEIR TERRITORY

BOTH ARE BAD AT ASKING _YOU_ QUESTIONS....

NEITHER TELLS YOU WHAT'S BOTHERING THEM

BOTH TEND TO SMELL RIPER WITH AGE

NEITHER DOES ANY DISHES

BOTH FART SHAMELESSLY

BOTH LIKE DOMINANCE GAMES

BOTH HAVE IRRATIONAL FEARS ABOUT VACUUM CLEANING

NEITHER KNOWS HOW TO TALK ON THE TELEPHONE

Chapter Three

WHY MEN ARE BETTER THAN DOGS

MEN ONLY HAVE <u>TWO</u> FEET THAT TRACK IN MUD

MEN CAN BUY YOU PRESENTS

MEN ARE A LITTLE BIT MORE SUBTLE

MEN DON'T EAT CAT TURDS ON THE SLY

MEN OPEN THEIR OWN CANS

DOGS HAVE DOG BREATH <u>ALL</u> THE TIME

MEN CAN DO MATH STUFF